A SLIGHT SHIFT IN THE AXIS

A SLIGHT SHIFT IN THE AXIS

Of Our Philosophical / Ethical Basis

James D. Littrell

4500 College Boulevard
Overland Park, Kansas 66211
888-888-7696
www.leatherspublishing.com

TABLE OF CONTENTS

A Religious Free Market Versus Totalitarianism

So it can't be proven to you that religion is man-made, even though you would have to admit that at least something on the order of 85 to 90 percent of what's out there called religion has to be manmade, providing that some portion of it were somehow genuine and divine. Can I get you to agree with that?

Now what if I could demonstrate to you that everything that has happened religiously appears to have come through normal or at least through some very typical human psychology? By that, at least you would then know that it might all be manmade, because that would show that there were reasons and motives behind it being both engendered and accepted — whatever sect of religion you would like to name. And Christians hate to be classified as a religion, by the way; that's degrading to them. They think they are above that. They don't want to be a part of anything that people can observe, test, or make general determinations about.

So if normal psychological motives can be assigned to everything religious that happened then at least that gives it the possibility of being manmade. The likelihood is there. It's possible. And so it's not only possible, it's perhaps even likely. You would have to admit that, or at least allow that as being possible.

Proving one form of religion or another through creation isn't going to work anymore. The more science closes in on evolutionary evidences the more apocalyptic some Christians may feel led to become in order to combat that, which is part of the Christian theological system's way to respond whenever its system is being threatened. So some Christians might make fools of themselves by becoming increasingly apocalyptic, provided that some will again take risks as if being led by the Spirit, and be bold enough to do so, despite how evangelical Christianity has allowed itself to rant and rave for quite some time now without it's people needing to take any prophetic risks — through dispensational theology, which became necessary so it could continue.

It's like I've said in a couple of other places: What disproves Christianity being divine doesn't concern creation, despite how Christian thinkers always use that as their chief defense and authorization for their system's philosophical existence. The thing that actually disproves it being divine has to do with its prophecies failing, by those not being powerful enough nor accurate enough, which shows it as something manmade after all, despite how a number of those prophecies did gain a degree of continuity by one Jewish prophet building on what another Jewish prophet had previously said or written in all of their national hopefulness, having their own national identity inherently tied to their deity's identity. This is not beyond our ability to sort this out now.

What's dangerous about Christianity is its apocalypticism, which Jim Jones and David Koresh so aptly demonstrated. For Christianity's moral assessments are only slightly skewed from what we need now, since (for example) only five of the Ten Commandments are relevant to this time, combined with a few other such realizations, when Christianity's authoritarianism can be laid aside long enough so that what's truly beneficial for us socially can be carefully considered.

So when you thoroughly assess the whole thing for what it is, instead of always pointing to creation, its real nature as something manmade will start to come through very loud and clear.

Another thing that also crosses it up by our day is how people cannot be held accountable with regard to its theological system — or in other words, be in real danger of or subject to the possibility of eternal hell — on a basis of something that has been gradually appearing more and more manmade. For how could a God put anyone in hell for eternity for simply suspecting that his religion might be manmade, whenever it is constantly appearing to be manmade? We are historical detectives now. We are detectives of everything now through our scientific advances, and nothing can really escape that. The truth is that Christianity's theological system, its interpretation of the world, is not being maintained by any sort of divinity. Only some new adherents instead keep popping up and trying to salvage it, seeking to make it still work, despite all of its problems. But enough already: We can do better now.

And just because someone like the evangelist Charles Stanley came along and sort of saved the day for evangelical Christianity right after Protestantism's very serious church chaos of the 1970's and 80's, that still doesn't change what Christianity essentially is; nor do such efforts change several of Christianity's basic characteristics that are tending to become more and more problematic for us now.

Take Catholicism for instance, Christianity's earliest and most predominant organized form. Catholicism has been incredibly totalitarian historically. No one can deny that; it's like the nose on your face. And this demonstrates a huge philosophical problem with Christianity, one that goes back to the roots of its conception philosophically. Here is the problem: If the religion does not become universal then it won't work. What I mean by that is this: If you allow people to choose their own philosophy or religion freely then too many of them will always choose something else instead of what's been made the officially accepted interpretive system. Catholicism's Inquisition of the 1300's demonstrates that. PBS recently ran a program on the Inquisition and Catharism. And Catharism was only one of the alterative forms of religion that the Catholics took such a totalitarian stance against historically. Consider also, that when the Catholics killed those people, they thought they might be helping to save the Cathar's souls, at least that was in the minds of many who were doing the killing and torturing. But the truth is, when Constantine declared Christianity the official religion of the Roman Empire in the fourth century, going back some one thousand years before the time of the Inquisition, the killing of people who didn't convert became essential at that much earlier time also. If authoritarian religion doesn't become universal then it cannot be what it was designed to be, which could lead to a free market of ideas, and therefore some influences that would undermine it philosophically, since it would then be forced to compete on a level playing field — something Christianity doesn't truly allow for philosophically, nor accept. Even that idea alone would overturn its main philosophical assumptions. Likewise, when you give the ignorant masses the freedom to think they will very often come up with malarkey anyway, since some people are always trying to trick other people to get more influence, or perhaps more women, or more power or whatever. The inclination of men is to be selfish, and their motives in philosophy aren't always much better. Creating something disciplined and accurate isn't necessarily our tendency. But we eventually will be forced to seek for that by the chaos that's been created by all of our forerunner's philosophical mistakes. So this is a historical process, and hopefully one that we are paying attention to. And we don't need to catch a ride on any more comets that will be coming by either.

In evangelical Christianity, it is their apocalyptic scenario that becomes the totalitarian component, which ends up providing for that killing of anyone and everyone that doesn't conform (essentially like the

Catholics at it's most basic level), except in evangelicalism's case this is to come later and in the future, which allows it to remain authoritarian and totalitarian — a totalitarian component that will eventually put all of its non-conformers into an eternal hell. That is the nature of authoritarian religion: It has an incredible need to be totalitarian. It doesn't even exist without that. It's main premise would fail and it would lose its logical ability to explain the universe and how everything works.

And so evangelicalism does this also, by transferring all of its totalitarianism into the future vengeance of God through its apocalypticism. Become a good evangelical, get into it deeply regarding what the Bible really states, and it will take you there. It is simply the nature of the beast, and one that many liberal churches have tried very hard to change or diminish, but without any genuine success. Anyone who doesn't simply use the Bible for his or her own self-determined aims will be led there by it. We have minds and we have words, and those words have meanings. Spend enough time in the Bible, and its preponderance will become very obvious. Many of today's ministers may continue to put out the Bible's radical apocalyptic fires for their simpleminded flocks, if that's what their people want them to do, and so make their parishioners days and weeks into nice ones philosophically. But for those who immerse themselves in the Bible, and for those who wish to take it all in completely: Watch out! You will be taking on its cause, which is ultimately the cause of that precarious Nation of Israel after David and Solomon's time, transferred over to Jesus of Nazareth as its promised deliverer, something that was transformed into a somewhat paradoxical nonviolent mode, yet retaining its totalitarian deliverance of the Israel Nation, nonetheless, as it meanwhile tries to sweep up a ton of gentiles and spread influence through its apocalyptic all-encompassing program (which has ended up working remarkably well as a business, provided its people will keep missing most of its insecure Jewish apocalyptic fundamentals).

All of this is a labyrinth, and one of the most difficult type to sort out. It's almost impossible to sort out, in fact. It's almost over our heads. It was made, it was devised, to be over our heads. Discovering it to be manmade was never meant to happen. It's a combination of quixotic sincere believers and thoughtfully helpful Machiavellians throwing in together in an historic effort encompassing many centuries. Whatever other writings came along or were produced in the same vein, but didn't make the cut, simply weren't included lest this system be embarrassed for what it really is. Only the more sophisticated pieces that helped bolster its mystical monotheism were included and compiled. Religious leaders in our past needed authority over the masses and a way to explain the world. That is what this is. It was compiled in a way to never be overturned. What seemed right and necessary historically for mankind socially was incorporated. Men thought long and hard to solve theological and social problems through this religious conduit. But it's manmade and so won't quite do the trick in our day, not as long as it pretends to be anything other than what it really is.

So please don't become one of those that tries to save the day for this system. Just let it go. Follow our academics instead. I tried that and spent the better portion of 30 years of my life trying to understand and break through in that way. Take it from me, please: It won't work. God won't be there for you to validate anything. If anything seems to be so, it's simply you being romantic about it and interpreting it to be so. Mere chance offers that sort of potential a lot more often than we might think. And when you convince yourself to believe something, your mind can also play tricks on you. We don't need anyone to become apocalyptic now. We should instead streamline our lives and make our families' environments more happy ones, while helping our country to be a better one and do our part in the world. Even with no life after death that still makes plenty of sense.

That need for hoped-for and interpreted interactions with a deity through mysticism isn't proving to be nearly so helpful now.

Not For The Jews Nor Anyone Else

Becoming a Christian has gradually turned into an initiation process. Not that it didn't have its initiation by baptism originally; it did. It just sort of morphed some more by our day. And turning something like this into a one-time thing is just a natural tendency of ours anyway. People always want to make anything and everything easier if they can. It's human nature to do so.

The evangelical initiation into Christianity today involves a belief in Jesus, and very often walking an aisle and then praying a prayer of confession and devotion, usually followed by baptism. But the New Testament tries to say that there is quite a bit more to being a real Christian than just that. Nevertheless, this is what becoming a Christian now involves, at least when it comes to being an evangelical type Christian.

I would like to illustrate a couple of problems with the Christian philosophy that I am now ashamed of. I was one of those that took in all of the teachings, instructions, and admonitions found in the New Testament. And I tried to obey them all, and so not just make being a Christian into a one-time initiation process only. And some could think that what I did was very devoted and, therefore, better. But I'm going to try to explain to you some of the pitfalls in that, because men are the ones who actually came up with all of this, and in a time when understanding our world wasn't nearly as developed or thorough as it is now. And many Christians may want to complain that we have now made things worse because most people no longer just swallow all of the Bible's proclamations as being flawlessly divine, because so many more of us are observers and testers of things now. We don't swallow things too easily now if and when they don't really hold water. And so morally better or not, most of us want what is really accurate now. And the moral part we can work on, to make our world a better place, and to make all of our lives generally happier. Threatening people with hell isn't the only way to get people to turn from stupidity, and to instead embrace what is good.

I absorbed a couple of problems from the New Testament in the course of being so disturbed by the religious chaos of the 1970's and 80's, and so took on an unusual religious devotion to find the right way through all of that. I'm actually somewhat ashamed of that now, for my not being more normal because of all of this. But you have to understand how disturbed I was by all of that religious chaos. It was a big problem, and I wanted to get to the bottom of it — if I could. And the only way to get to the bottom of that was through an unusual religious devotion, to see if this was everything that it has been claiming to be, which it finally and completely proved not to be, from my viewpoint.

The best way to illustrate all of this is by going directly to the words of Christ in the New Testament, something Paul said were for all of us (everyone) in

1 Timothy 6:3. I want you to see the real cynicism and pessimism of the New Testament.

Dispensationalism, that vastly predominant theology of modern evangelicals, doesn't allow for using the words of Christ that much or applying them. Evangelicalism uses Christ as a sacrifice for sin, and not really so much as a theological instructor. And evangelicals are the ones who have made Christianity into an initiation process above and beyond anything else now, instead of more closely following everything that the New Testament teaches — indications about someone's real spiritual status being realized by how a person lives his or her life, things the Gospels (Jesus' words) stress as being so incredibly important. And so it's actually good for you to know that this is all manmade now, believe it or not, so that you and your children won't be tempted to become disturbed as in the way I became about all of this, so that more people can live out their lives in a more tranquil condition, and so much more in the way they would do normally, provided they are knowledgeable enough to realize that good behavior is rewarding for everyone, both in honor and happiness, in and of itself.

I want to warn you about some places in the Gospels that tell people to bypass worries that have to do with being normal. One place has a man wanting to follow Jesus, but first he wanted to bury his father. Jesus told him to "let the dead bury their dead" (Matthew 8:21), which might seem reasonable under the circumstances, except for how meditating on such a saying can lead some Christians into a somewhat pessimistic philosophical slant. One thing that a person can subliminally absorb philosophically from that is a belief that everyone else beside Christians are "dead," which initially shows a degree of arrogance and disrespect, and so carries with it a certain cynical tone. This verse also seems disrespectful toward the normal practice of people being concerned with their loved ones at the ends of their lives, and sort of seems to trivialize our normal burial formalities also, perhaps as something temporal and so not really all that worthy of our time. So not only do I find the New Testament's teachings on demons problematic to young people, I think this can also be somewhat misleading philosophically to some of them, and might even short circuit some very natural and normal human sensitivities. So even though this kind of a teaching might help religious followers to be more devoted, it doesn't help young people assimilate into society all that well. And since it's so radical sounding, most people haven't really ever listened all that much to this segment, and so it gets sort of passed over in the Bible, except by those who want to become more fully devoted, those who try to understand or absorb the Bible author's mindsets — something many mothers have typically been in favor of, not realizing that there is a potential for some ideological harm to their children from the New Testament.

Perhaps the Christian Religion found it necessary to go to those sorts of extremes on occasion, in order to reach enough people, in order to get them to react or be affected. But for society in the long run, such radical teachings aren't really all that helpful, not at all. So what this religion may have needed in order to get off the ground has ended up not being all that good for us in the long haul. And if there was only one verse like that then we might overlook it as merely an aberration, but there are several more that are quite similar.

It just so happens that Matthew, Mark, Luke, and John are the books that everyone has become accustomed to as containing the things Christ said. Yet in reality, there may be some variations between what is found there and what Jesus actually spoke. But quibbling over that now probably won't help us. Even if people like Matthew, Mark, and Luke helped what Jesus said to some degree, what we have in the Bible's Gospels is still adequate enough to be put to a test, with all of the time and history that has now passed, so that we can see how all of those really apply and work. Therefore, we may as well treat all of those as if they are fairly accurate depictions of what Jesus said: For even if those contain some improvements over his exact sayings (which would make them some improved yet quixotic and hopeful manmade products, nonetheless, and so not actually divine) they will almost certainly become known as hopeful and quixotic statements eventually, despite whatever help may have been provided through those four theologians.

Another saying of Christ that's similar to the one about burying the dead has to do with taking regular measures when showing respect to a person's family (Luke 9:61). I know that Christians will try to argue in the Bible's defense that these are expressing the importance of becoming one of the twelve, or perhaps one of the other disciples that followed Jesus, or that it might apply to becoming a minister. But please bear in mind: The reality here is that Jesus diminishes the importance of some normal responsibilities that give a person a normal life and connectedness with the members of a person's family, perhaps even with the world itself, to some extent. If being connected in that way is diminished whatsoever, it can contribute to some anti-social thinking, particularly in our young people which can lead to some long-lasting cynicism toward the world generally, which is not good if that becomes overly pronounced — something that has far too often been deeply accepted.

Many of the words in the New Testament are ascetic like this and call for extremes and loss of sensitivity. Doing so is also a tactic used in brainwashing, believe it or not. And there are many such places in the New Testament that invoke this sort of asceticism (1 John 2:15, John 12:25, Luke 14:33, Luke 14:26, Luke 9:23, Mark 10:21, Mark 8:34, Matthew 10:37-39, Matthew 6:19-20).

If something was really urgent and required sacrifice, that is understandable. But if that idea has now proven to have been mistaken, then the teaching of ongoing cynicism toward the world is counter productive and uncalled for. All I'm saying is, that such sayings can contribute to a person adopting a philosophical approach that diminishes the importance of their life, their family, and their profession, as well as their ancestors. And so those sayings have actually turned out to have been sort of a power play — a power play for what was thought would become an apocalyptic moment or event, except didn't.

Once again, there is nothing wrong with a temporary test of loyalty if something is deemed so important, as long as a person knows that such a test is temporary. But with Christianity's "love not the world neither the things that are in the world," "hate your own life," "forsake all," "hate your father, mother, wife, children, brethren," "deny yourself," and "let the dead bury the dead," it's possible for a young person to adopt a pessimistic, or even a lax, casual, and cynical worldview that diminishes the only life that he or she will ever have, instead of enhancing it. (A couple of these last six quoted phrases are slightly paraphrased.)

Is A Religion With No Authoritarian
Teeth Possible?

Perhaps what we need is to let a religion evolve, so that as we learn more and more we can be incorporating what we learn into that religion — change it when and where it needs changing, and then put Jesus' name on top of it all, and so give it a Christian identity.

But hey, that's exactly what modern Christianity is right now! And so it's become somewhat confusing because some of us haven't yet realized that that is exactly what the most prevalent form of evangelical Christianity presently is. But regarding me personally, had a church that I became associated with (after our church split) not done a series of messages on the fear of God, some 30 odd years ago, then perhaps I, too, would have gone on in the Christian Religion like many others, just a little more naturally, as though everything about Christianity in relation to the world was meant to be, so that where it might not seem to fit real well on occasion could have just seemed like some slight idiosyncrasy that could for the most part be overlooked. And so perhaps I would have thought, like many Christian still do, that people interacting with God through Christianity's initiation process as the chief among all life aspects. But then you would always have those old Bible loyalist stickler people trying to both find and point out where people have been getting off track, as they show the contrast between what the Bible says and how things are now. So perhaps my wishful philosophical harmony might have lasted just at a little longer, yet it was still destined to find some eventual molestation.

If we want a religion now, and we want Jesus' name stamped on it as its religious identity, then I don't have a problem with that. The only problem comes in when we become duplicitous about it so that we won't admit what we're doing. But that is caused by the nature of this religion being authoritarian. It needs people to be afraid of it and reverence it. It needs to say, "This is the way things are, and everyone needs to respond to this. This is universal and true." And on that count Christianity has now failed, by the way, or it will be failing in the eyes of many more not too far in the future.

And so it's a paradox. People like religion. People need religion, not all but most of us. Or we at least all need to have an understanding and some explanations regarding our world. And we definitely need an ethical system as well. And it's those kinds of explanations and ethics that the Christian Religion has been a conduit of.

Therefore, can we know that our religion is man-made, and still, nevertheless, keep it? Can it still be beneficial to us and effective like that? So can it still do for us what we need it to? Would we still be decent human beings to each other? Would we still look out for the poor? Or would we all become arrogant s.o.b.'s whenever certain of us become successful? So will we all act like, "You can't touch this," as if certain of us have become such evolutionary pieces of work? And so will we then pass by the man who fell among thieves, if no one but us would know whether we passed by in a rush? Or would we still become Good Samaritans, just for the sake of our own self-worth and happiness, so that we aren't just a bunch of cynical and predictable self-absorbed sticks in the mud? Despite how God isn't standing there with a stick in his hand ready to strike us, or to perhaps put us in hell, or else reward us in a life after death? So will we still bend ourselves over backwards for other people sometimes? Simply because, if we were in their same predicament, we would want them to do the same thing for us?

So what is it then that we love so much about Christianity? Is it the life after death? Is it the salvation from hell and eternity in heaven? Or is it instead all of those stories that that tell us to be heroes simply for the sake of being heroes, when no one is looking? Simply for ourselves and for that person we are being good to? Simply because we believe in the worthwhileness of life and we believe in what we essentially are (which includes the other people in our world), and what we ought to be or should become?

And then what about sex? How in the world are we going to handle that? Now that certain aspects of sodomy are practiced between so many couples these days, as if by routine and without many deterrents to prevent it? The definition of sodomy has now changed, by the way, from two or three distasteful alternative sex acts into anal or oral sex that is forced — a change that seems to have been affected by our present understanding of science, the body, illness, risks, and hygiene, etc. And so what is bad in sex and what's good then? What is off limits and what's okay? And can all of this work in a religion that knows it has no real authoritarian teeth left? Or in a culture that becomes completely secular?

The answer is yes, it can work, just like the guy that knows that no God is watching him but still and instinctively he becomes a Good Samaritan, because he loves himself and life more for doing that. His happiness is greater through that, even though he will probably take on a certain amount of trouble by doing so. And when he looks at himself in the mirror he likes what he sees a whole lot more because of that. He (she) feels that there is a greater purpose in life than simply beating out the competition 24-7-365. In fact, without that I don't think we can really be happy, at least not all that deeply. And religion has been the means to take us there. So we have to give religion that: It has made us think — a lot.

No, we can do sex just fine today. We can. And we can do it under the same religion-influenced format. And Catholics can keep being Catholics if they wish to. We can handle that. We can do this just fine. And Protestant Churches can keep immersing or sprinkling also if they want, and keep teaching the lessons of Jesus. The landscape wouldn't have to drastically change.

There will never be a day when good homes aren't needed. That's why it's important that our younger people form bonds that lead to marriages, ones that will last their whole lifetimes. There is no better way to live and be happy than to find the person that you ought to be with, make a permanent connection, then protect, keep, and nourish that, and so live out your lives together. And the children raised in such a happy setting will typically become very special. This is part of us being what we ought to be as well, and it has to do with sex, as surprising as some may find that. It's all connected. What's good for us all socially has a deep sexual component. What's best for us just doesn't fall off a log. Good families and sexual behavior are connected. The best scenario, both personally and culturally, should be encouraged by our society and in our culture. A monogamous, faithful, heterosexual family unit should always be king among all of the sexual possibilities. Life is about much more than just sex: It's about families and homes also. And it seems that many of us might need to become more aware of that.

A sexual partner has the right to expect fidelity. If a person can't provide that sort of fidelity under a certain circumstance, then some honest communication should take place. We should all keep in mind that married monogamous homes are the real social engine behind a rather large well-oiled human machine. Sorry to step on a few progressive toes by that, but the day we can come back around to at least admitting that will be the same day we will reach a realistic compromise on all of this. If we take down or dismantle married monogamous life-long relationships that produce families as the ideal, we will also take down and dismantle what is best for us as humans. Moving toward more radical change, without this compromise, isn't in our species' best interest.

Alternatives happen. Yet alternatives don't have to be the ideal. Tolerance and acceptance of alternatives is one thing; idolizing all things as being socially equivalent isn't in our best interest over all. Everyone can't be the star. Life happens. Stuff happens. Not everyone gets to be a role model.

And so alternative sexual situations will happen. So will those people who defer to some of those alternatives go to hell then? No, they will not. And so should they be punished somehow for not practicing what is our ideal? No they shouldn't, not unless some of them, in the process of doing so, cloud or take away the happy future of a child, or damage that child's potential in the world. We will never accommodate children being the prey to any of our adult's sexual appetites. To think that there are some people out there who don't get this, that some don't understand how there is a difference between sex with a child and another adult, is disgusting. That is elementary school ethics. People don't marry off their daughters at the age of twelve anymore, in order to keep from having to feed them. We live in a different world from the past. Without our social regulations, life as we know it wouldn't be possible. And there are thousands of laws and regulations to follow that didn't exist in the recent past. The fact that we have now defined what's proper for our children sexually should be no surprise to anyone. And we will take over where any parents drop the ball, if we need to. This is who we are today. None of this is surprising. Raping a child is what's surprising. We tend to put ourselves in the child's shoes; why wouldn't we? Children aren't the property of others who are older and more powerful. Children have rights, rights to have the expectations of some respectful treatment and protection as they are growing up.

Homosexuality is an alternative sexual behavior also, and one that we can't prevent from happening. And though it will happen, I wouldn't ever recommend teaching it as being equivalent to our ideal in our schools. There is obviously no way to enforce universal heterosexuality. Doing so would be totalitarian. People can be gay if they want to be, and apparently live out some long and productive lives while doing so, even though a lot of us hard-nosed redneck heterosexuals have not wanted to have to realize that. But we have to go with the reality and simply encourage the ideal in the midst of being tolerant. And I don't mean reluctantly tolerant, I mean respectfully tolerant. This is a realistic compromise: Everyone is going to have to give a little. People have the freedom to be gay if they want to be, and meanwhile have all of the respect within every facet of life that other productive citizens receive. But we don't need to start envisioning an increasingly gay or bisexual world because of that. Gay activists are much like activists in the abortion debate: None of the sides are ever satisfied as they always want more, whether more is actually good for us socially or not. The next cool thing in the world is not turning everyone into a bisexual, or creating more sexual promiscuity. Most of us are naturally too sexual already.

Divorce is another thing, and it's going to keep happening now as well. But perhaps divorce will decrease as fewer and fewer couples get married, since the social pressures to tie the knot have now decreased by quite a lot. Virginity is no longer the ideal that it once was, not in this culture. And if you are going to try to speak to the American public in the future, you will have to learn this and adapt. This is simply how things are now. Marriage has both economic and emotional risks. Birth control is now very prevalent. Having marriages that truly ought to happen is more preferable. Our society has already gone there, and is still going there. It will work. It will be okay. No Christian revival will ever reverse this. That's a pipe dream now. Christians can be perpetually miserable about that and contend for the ideals of the past, as those once stood in the past; or they can accept this and go on with the rest of us now.

Kids raised without two parents, or in a situation with divorced parents, will miss out on some of the social luxuries they could have had. That's just the way it is. Many children will overcome this handicap, but far more will carry some sort of handicap from that misfortune into their future. We need to keep that in mind wherever having a child is a potential. Like I said, sex has all kinds of implications above and beyond the mere sex act. The better we realize that, the fewer problems we will create for ourselves — problems that affect us all.

A home with two parents that love each other is the ideal. And it's not just the children that miss out; the parents miss out on things as well whenever that doesn't happen. It's too bad that not more of us find that, but that's the reality. Many of us won't be able to obtain that. So the social ideal of the past — a faithful, monogamous, heterosexual, loving marriage — simply isn't possible for each and every one of us, even though it should still be the ideal. The only difference is that we should be more tolerant of those who resort to some alternatives now. We don't need to be totalitarian about our ideals now. We can now do both: We can hold what's ideal as we tolerate what is not our ideal, simultaneously. It's a compromise. It's one that makes sense. I think it will be good for us. I think it will work well.

So alternative situations will come into play. But this time I am no longer speaking about the alternative of the gay lifestyle. I am now speaking about some heterosexual alternatives: serial monogamy through multiple divorces or a series of relationships encompassing multiple partners over time, sexual dating, even multiple partners simultaneously will also happen on certain rare occasions. But those are contracts of confidence between individuals. No one can actually regulate that. Some of that will happen. People will try things. Everyone is unique and has unique circumstances. When an adult realizes that he or she has made a mistake, it is he or she that will have to bring that mistake to an end, in this day and in our culture. Every adult is responsible for his or her own sexual behavior. Society can teach and encourage the ideal, and do some damage control work, but the personal freedom to choose one's own course and sexual lifestyle is part of a person being allowed to live the life he or she chooses, as long as it's legal and doesn't injure someone else.

Stuff happens, life happens, the ideal isn't going to work for everyone. Let's frame all of this as it really is. Let's look at the whole picture. Young people, young adults, can make their own choices about all of this.

Authoritarian religion isn't going to work any longer. So is there really a God? There doesn't appear to be, but it's still possible. And if one is there then I'm afraid it might be somewhat akin to The Force in Star Wars perhaps. Personally, I no longer believe in the existence of any interactive deity, yet I understand religious people and what they need. And I think I understand what our society needs also when it comes to ethical behavior and human interactions. Does that make me perfect? No. This just happens to be what I have spent a lot of my time thinking about, while comparing many real life notes, disappointments, frustrations, and a few successes. It's interesting how life's difficulties can sometimes speak more philosophically than many of those things that come off with virtually no problem. I learn at the table of hard knocks fairly often.

As far as religion, we can keep as much of it as people want to keep. We can do whatever we want. We are all free; no one is telling us what we must do. If a religion can continue under its present market format, then it will probably continue. If people require it to be altered, yet want it to continue, then it will be altered and continue. If being purely secular becomes more attractive, then very many will do that. But Jesus did teach a number of really great things; and we ought to keep the best of that within our thinking both now and in the future. But we can meanwhile lay off several of those more problematic Bible sections. And cherishing the things of our history, which includes our religious history, why wouldn't we want to do that? We can handle all of this. We can evolve.

Religious people can disregard all of this and try to say that all of this isn't so. And our society can continue to look for its moral guides from among those who have their heads in the sand, from those who aren't fully aware. Or we can acknowledge what's happened and prepare to deal with all of this realistically and straightforwardly. Or perhaps we can instead just keep hoping that by applying pressure in one direction, that the law of averages will cause people to be hung out to dry somewhere in the middle morally and philosophically, and so not necessarily by their conscious choice but through intimidation. But that isn't accurate, honest, nor comprehensive, when we are finally forced to consider each and every aspect of this together. So it seems better for us to obtain and hold our children's respect and trust continuously now, as we bring them along, rather than resort to coercing them about any of this through guilt. Life isn't a cute little cameo for each and every one of us.

So can we retain some special respect for the heterosexual family unit then? All of us? Or must a very large number of us remain authoritarian Christians, continue worrying about hell and freaking out about sex, in order to keep what's best for our majority, and keep that moving ahead and into our future?

The Nature of Evil

Theologians who wrote the books that became a part of the Bible theorized that the thing which causes evil in the world arises from lust, a combination of lust and unbelief actually. The apostle Paul once wrote (in Romans 7) that he would have "not known what coveting really was if the law had not said 'Do not covet.' But sin, seizing the opportunity afforded by the commandment, produced in me (him) every kind of covetous desire. For apart from the law, sin is dead." He goes on to say that, "Once I was alive apart from the law; but when the commandment came, sin sprang to life and I died" And then finally, "For sin, seizing the opportunity afforded by the commandment, deceived me, and through the commandment put me to death" (Rom.7:7-11 NIV). And so an authoritarian commandment against something can sometimes intensify the desire or lust to do whatever is thought bad or off limits.

So why is that? And is Paul's take on this the very best and most accurate explanation for what's really going on psychologically with all of this?

A thing that the Christian philosophy fails to recognize quite well enough has to do with what actually constitutes something being evil. And the thing that makes something evil is reason, which Christianity attempts to recognize somewhat also, except that it fails in doing so by indirectly violating that, which is an unavoidable principle. It works kind of like this: Christianity says that something is evil for such and such reason, and then adds that sometimes it's only God who really understands what some of those reasons are. And so his commandments become sort of a stopgap between what's evil and what people should do instead, which has been simplified for people by God giving some instructions and prohibitions through his commandments and laws. Therefore, Christianity says that God's commandments provide what people need, first to make people realize they have a problem, and then secondly Christianity explains what people need to change in their behavior and thinking. Christianity then provides explanations about how people can be reconciled to God through faith as well, so that people can be in a new faith relationship with God that is further facilitated through some explanations about redemption as it claims to restore believers to something that was allegedly lost (the potential for people to interact with God), something that's reinstated from a person's Christian conversion forward. Yet all of this is nothing but philosophical callisthenics that can be explained in a much easier way.

Even though a good deal of this has appeared to make some sense, as though this could be true or real, it's our need for guidance and ethics that gives it that appearance. And many theologians have, indeed, carefully weighed and thought through quite a lot of this; so this isn't something that has been casually put together. Plus this system does tend to help many to become some slightly better behaved citizens fairly often also, despite Christianity's good dose of hype and pessimistic apocalypticism.

Yet here is what seems to be really going on. Mere ignorance (the need for information and understanding), the thing that every child initially comes into the world possessing an ample share of, is enough to cause a great number of us to make several grave mistakes and wrong choices. So pray tell, what is so incredibly mysterious about that!? Why do we need any of those longer or more elaborate explanations over and above this?

The real reason why something becomes more attractive when it's made off limits has to do with humans being exactly what we are, some extraordinarily adaptable and curious beings. Adaptability and curiosity — that ability to become intelligent — is what has enabled humanity to become such an extraordinarily successful species. And it's not just our natures to be so, this goes way back in time where the payoff came through different types of rewards that were realized or obtained through this kind of creativity. It is our nature to explore things and learn things, which once helped our ancestors survive, something that in more recent times has sort of collided into a brick wall after some authoritarian religious commands came into play.

We still have a deep desire to test anything and everything in order to see if something is really what someone says it is, in order to see if it's instead some sort of self-seeking trick that someone is trying to hoodwink us through. While growing up, the simple process of children interacting with other children causes most of us to see many examples of that. We learn about human psychology early on by interacting with other self-seeking children. To be so is our nature; this is extremely typical. Therefore, most of us acquire an acute awareness of that potential.

And so most of us will suspect that some adults may do some conniving a little later in life as well, something that more than a few grownups have obliged by doing. And suspecting people like this can become so natural to us that we may wonder whether our religious leaders might pull a few strings on occasions also, or perhaps simply make some mistakes. It's our nature to question things. So resenting a commandment doesn't necessarily mean that a person is a slave to sin.

It is true that any person can adopt any one in a number of bad habits that can preoccupy him or her with some malevolent control or addiction. People can even become self-destructive through certain deficiencies or personal ignorance, and through some bad decisions or risk-taking. Yet that doesn't mean anyone has a pact with the devil or sin. Every bit of this, all of it, comes through nothing but ignorance.

And so what the apostle Paul said, concerning the commandment intensifying the desire for something, can be explained very simply in this way instead, as part of an evolutionary and, therefore, rather visceral survival instinct, which means it doesn't necessarily come through any type of moral degeneracy. The apostle Paul, by adopting that approach (which wasn't so incredibly far off, by the way), provided a way for the ancient Jewish religious system to sort of keep its theory regarding life and existence going. Christianity builds on some early Jewish theological basics, yet colors in many more details and answers, all of which enable the old system to continue, along with its deity, which underlies its national identity. Paul accommodated all of that through his explanations of how Christianity works.

Another thing involved with this concerns how some of the Judeo-Christian prohibitions (desires termed evil) happen to be some very strong desires that typical people come by quite naturally, whether it's the desire to have valuable things, sex, or to release some anger through rage. All of that is natural yet has to be limited. And commandments were some of men's first courses of action to take against excesses or misbehaviors related to these kinds of desires. Even today, there are commandments all around us, not divine commandments but governmental ones, that have been made to protect us from each other and make our lives much more predictable.

What makes something evil is reason. If something doesn't actually hurt someone, and if people want to do it, if it doesn't carry some subtle deleterious affect, then whatever it is, it isn't evil. Reason is what makes something evil. If you can demonstrate enough strong reasons, show how something can't be tolerated or allowed, and can also demonstrate the hideousness of something or the wrong motives or reasons behind it, then you have exposed something that's evil — evil which is certainly still alive and well in our time.

And then there is the argument that some might make about how survival may sometimes require a choice between oneself and someone else, or between one clan or group of people and another, as if one of those should survive and another shouldn't. But no one really wants to live in a world like that. Even the people who would kill others to procure what they believe is necessary can now lose their own reason for living through that. What worked in our ancient past won't always transfer to now. Yet such things demonstrate a strong visceral power and instinct very often, perhaps just a little too often. What worked back then won't necessarily work now. We simply aren't in every way what our species once was. Many things have changed. We have evolved, our minds have evolved: What once worked won't necessarily work now. And though much of that will still come to the surface on occasion, as something that was once more vital during our species' past, a good deal of that won't work in the way it once did. We don't kill and eat our enemies now, for example. And most people no longer traverse near the brink of their own survival these days. Advanced civilization is what rules during this time.

Unfortunately, some of the world's people still aren't thinking in the terms of our present evolution though. Some of them would even like to rearrange the power structure of our world. Some would like to shake things up and bring things down, hoping they could arise as much more powerful figures in the aftermath of our civilization's collapse. What a shame it would be if we ever allow such people to take over the world. There are influences out there much worse than Christianity, influences that would like to see such a revamping. Christian apocalyptic hopes are sheepish in comparison.

What presently exists right now is the most tolerant and the most open-minded system ever. It is also a system with the most diversity and acceptance of all time, one that makes more people happy simultaneously than the world heretofore has ever known. You can call it a disappointment, even evil, if you would like, I think this is an incredibly good realistic attempt.

And so evil is usually equated with ignorance in some way, misguided ignorance, ignorance gone wild in some insane direction. Loving others as ourselves is the rule of the day: Anything else is evil. And it would be better to die than to live if raping, killing, or pillaging your neighbor was the only way to survive. If we must compromise a life principle in order to survive then such survival becomes much less worthwhile. Better to go down with dignity together as a human family than to kill your neighbor in order to make your own life last a short moment longer, which can make everything that remains rather tainted or regretful. Helping one another when things are dire is much more in character with how we now fancy ourselves — an essential human trait for our time.

For now, whenever it comes down to killing or being killed, a person or country might sometimes have to kill if serious danger from another is imminent. Nevertheless, in a world like ours and in a time like this, preserving the lives of all of our fellow humans ought to be our rule for the day. Therefore, we have to hope for better things now, more widespread trust, more sharing of causes, and more understanding of each other. Killing and war has become unpopular, and rightfully so. It would be best if we all had no enemies, but the reality is that we do. Struggling against evil, and the ignorance that nurtures a particular evil, can lead us to make some difficult or perhaps even questionable decisions. But where genuine allocation for peaceful coexistence is advocated and maintained then some degree of necessary killing and war must be tolerated as sometimes being necessary. Sacrificing yourself to villains with a vision isn't the same as going down with your friends. For now, war remains a fact of life, as regretful as that is. Yet if something such as resources should ever run low, then the burden of that shortage should be spread wide and felt by us all.

Nothing is absolutely perfect, but we have to live with ourselves. We can't just paint over something to make it easier on ourselves. Our consciences won't allow that. Part of living is having a mindset that is poised to enjoy it. We are very complex creatures now, and what makes us happy is rather complex as well. If a person's cause and purpose is pure deep down then a person should know that within his or her heart. And so motives revert back, first to what was intended, and then secondly to available information, which can afford some degree of tolerance for mistakes. None of this is easy, nor will most people let themselves off easily. Many times people are harder on themselves than they ought to be, just as quite a few aren't nearly as hard on themselves as they should be. But it's good that most people take doing what's right very seriously.

It's not really all that hard to adopt some righteous anger, or what some may believe is righteous anger. Anger, by the way, is still needed to some extent. But improperly supported anger, which can be improportionate in its viciousness, is evil also. And so stupidity, in no matter what form it takes on, simply can't win.

Being lazy and stupid is a double hit, especially since laziness may be stupidity's biggest contributor. But there are a lot of ways to be stupid and maybe about half that many ways to be evil. But even governments can become stupid, and once in a while even evil. Religions are not automatically exempt from this either, by the way. Everything will be weighed in the balance of humanity's collective intelligence. And it's that intelligence which will determine what's evil and what's good, who deserves some historical praise and who deserves some level of scorn, according to what was known at the time — after things have had time to settle.

The Cradle of Eternity

One of the worst problems, if not the worst problem of all, with deciding that there is no interactive deity overseeing us, has to do with our need to be nurtured and cared for. That's just the way life is: It needs to be cradled somehow, even as life in earth's warm oceans is cradled, as precipitation watering the land imbues it with plants and animals also, even as the tempered rays from the sun almost perfectly energize it all.

It's not easy to think that all of this happens without intelligent oversight. To think that seems out of whack with how things work in our environment. When things happen on earth it's usually some intelligent thing or being that has chosen to do something. Randomness seems heartless; nobody wants it. We want God to be there and to also be affected by us. We like to think that we can have that kind of impact on our own wellbeing, our survival and our future. We need a deity to cradle us. So we hope he is there and listening. And whenever he doesn't seem to pay attention, surely it's our fault in some way, and so never his fault or that his super intelligence and oversight simply doesn't exist.

Eternity is like that also. We think that minds that are so incredibly aware surely couldn't be temporary. Something that has become this developed and complex surely couldn't be cast aside one day as though it were worthless. Surely everything goes on forever!

And surely we will be there in that state of eternity forever — somehow.

And even if not, wouldn't it be better to think of it in such a way anyway? Regardless of whether it is true or not? So what really happens eventually isn't as important as us feeling safe and secure or loved and cradled in time and space now. It's what we need to live. Part of that is seeing ourselves cradled and held in eternity also. We want our existence to accommodate what we have become, creatures with minds so large that we can observe and consider almost anything out there with a fairly good hope of fathoming it.

But how many other creatures out there are also observing and postulating about their surroundings? All things that live, whether in the most basic of all forms or in some of those higher animal forms, deal with all sorts of problems that concern their survival. And so will each and every one of those come back to have an existence in eternity also? And so where would the cutoff be then, in relation to sophistication? Life that prowls or is cute gets included while life such as ants, worms, or most insects is cast aside and forgotten?

I know the answer. Only God knows. Right? Only God has known a lot of things in the recent past. We simply need him to be there, and that's why he is there. His existence is the product of a sophisticated mind that needs to be cradled in every single thing it can fathom. And so eternity became another problematic thing.

But here is the real question for us. Is the scenario we have created to address and provide for that psychological security, will that prove to be a significant handicap if it isn't true or accurate? Or can we continue soothing ourselves with all of that without any derogatory consequences from such a falsehood?

And when determining the potential validity of any religious belief, should that be done alone through abstract concepts of logic? Or shouldn't we also go to a little more trouble of thoroughly assessing a religious system's historical claims, its performance, as well as its prophecies?

Making Heads and Tails of Protestants
and Catholics

Catholicism is a compromise. It tried to make something socially useful from all of what became the Christian traditions and beliefs, as leaders from the past tried to provide society with some very needed order, an order that prized ideological uniformity much more highly than we do now.

Therefore, Catholicism doesn't really try to be what Christianity was initially or what it was at its beginning — what we might term as pristine Christianity. Catholicism is instead a Christian adaptation to reality, the reality of everything that life went on to entail after that early Christian period gave way to more regular times. Catholicism doesn't even try hard at all to be what pristine Christianity was. It has instead tried to create an interpretation of that and so make out of that something that's more practical for all of the times that have followed.

The mistake that Protestantism makes is that it supposes that Bible Christianity is all that the early Christian writers portrayed it to be. But early Christianity was only what they said it was by believing it to be so, or at least by hoping that it was so. In reality, those early Christian writers actually hyped it quite a bit and made some really good sales presentations, or cases in defense of it. So it wasn't actually everything they hoped it was, nor was it actually everything they believed it to be.

And Protestantism is mistaken by supposing that pristine Christianity — Bible Christianity — is first of all possible, and then secondly that it's maintainable, which of course it isn't. Only hoping to make something that appears fairly similar is possible.

It is faith that makes that kind of Christianity possible. It is believing that all of that is happening which makes it sometimes seem like it's happening, which the human mind can do a very remarkable job with through its great ability to adapt or improvise in all sorts of situations and ways, in this case so Christians can get the desired interpretation from any event that occurs. Yet the Bible writers, too, set a lot of that ability up for the succeeding generations of Christians, having done so early on and in the first century, since they had to wrestle with those very same sort of difficulties — appearances of philosophical disjunction and failure. A big goal of Christianity is not simply to impose its ethical system, but to get everything that occurs to somehow fall harmoniously under its world-interpretation umbrella so that it never loses its appearance of validation by being miffed. The whole point is to believe it, and to also obtain everything that you might need from that belief, and then to keep all of that intact by continually finding things that might reinforce it.

It's sort of a philosophical game that Christians play. They sort of say: What has happened today that we can put in such a way that our belief system still looks valid? And how can we frame what has happened today so that our belief system isn't challenged? And those who become adept at such become masters for the Christian cause and its ethical system, which they feel is not just perfect but axiomatic. And though any Christian can play this game, it's usually the die-hard fundamentalist evangelicals that feel threatened enough to play it to this extent.

Catholics, in contrast, have their long tradition and its clergical system to rely on. Working on specifics that are more work/life related, and not so essentially philosophical, that is their typical area of devotion and expertise. Besides, Catholics don't need to fight for the legitimacy of that early or pristine Christianity, like so many evangelicals do, since Catholics believe it must have been God's intention all along that everything in the Church would be reshaped from what it initially started out being.

And Protestantism left Catholicism (during the Reformation) in order to revert back to the Bible — to the fundamentals and purity of everything that was pristine Christian. And our later generations have now typically lost track of this rather basic philosophical observation, since people don't usually think about what's really true all that much, only wanting what makes their own individual lives go more smoothly. People typically rally to anything and everything that makes their own lives smoother and better, no matter what, from whatever perspective they hold.

Protestantism's large historical split from the existing Church was founded upon a belief that Catholicism was impure, that Catholicism was a far-removed departure from all that was pristine Christian — that which the early church taught and practiced. And so what was written of that early time became the model, a model that Protestants hoped could be revived by following that pattern of whichever selected benchmarks they chose, which were found in the Bible, all of this following that time when the Christian scriptures became increasingly available to common folk in the succeeding generations after Wycliffe. But all of that Protestant hopefulness rests on this one supposition, that pristine Christianity is a real and ongoing possibility, which it isn't. Only different kinds of Christian social orders are actually possible.

Is Limiting Christian Belief Possible?

The answer to that is yes, a limited Christian belief is what most Christians hold. Yet there are some drawbacks with regard to attempting to limit it.

Christianity works fairly well as long as people refrain from believing it too much. And so a problem arises because Bible Christianity doesn't want its followers to only believe just a little bit. The Bible (Jesus also) is always calling for full commitment, which inevitably includes not only learning but also applying its apocalyptic aspects. And therein lies one of its biggest problems.

Sure, Christianity can make people pessimistic about the world because it teaches people that the world is evil, that it's sold under sin and the Devil, who is somehow capable of encircling the earth in the air with his band of demons to do war against God's angels whenever any political skirmishes arise on earth (Refer to Daniel chapter 10.). People who think the Bible is inerrant and perfectly divine have to swallow all of that. And so, number one, this belief can make you pessimistic.

The Christian belief can also make you into a mystic, where somehow or another you begin to believe that you might be able to interpret things that are happening within the spiritual realm all around you, which is rather subjective, wouldn't you say?

Christianity also turns some people into ascetics who try to gain control over their own fleshly desires and to also resist any vain or superfluous expressions that are made by anyone that doesn't follow their strict mode of conduct. It happens. There are still people like that who believe this is what God wants them to do, which actually deprives many by not furnishing them with quite enough reference points or perhaps enough experience or observations regarding certain things, which can sometimes produce even worse problems in the long run.

But laying aside all of that, perhaps the worst thing of all about Christianity has to do with its apocalypticism, which actually has an inherent ideological relation to that pessimism, mysticism, and asceticism. If a person becomes a Christian, if he or she feels sinful (which it very often encourages), and if they feel needy also, and if they take on the faith as the New Testament prescribes it, then they can very easily and eventually become apocalyptic kooks. And though many evangelical theologians are now trained to keep that from happening, to sort of tamp down that Bible influence and moderate it, to keep things sane, it is, nevertheless, still there and ready for some to absorb and then become bonkers over.

Therefore, can people then believe in Christianity only a little, and keep it that way, and in such a condition gain some real benefit? Yes, many do and it's possible. But if you come into the Christian faith in a very needy way, then look out!

Apocalyptic Christianity wants to remake the world through a second coming of Jesus. And it wants you to give up your life for him and for the future you will one day have if he raises you from the dead. It can also make you a better citizen here it appears, simply because it trains people to do all of that for Jesus' sake. Yet not every Christian becomes one of those sacrificial sheep ready for the slaughter. Some people build bunkers and shelters, and then store provisions and foodstuffs. And some have put together armories containing automatic and semiautomatic weapons in his behalf also. So look out.

Contact Information

leatherspublishing.com/theturningtide,
jdlittrell5@yahoo.com,

or

James D. Littrell
P.O. Box 32171
Kansas City, MO 64171

For numerous similar chapters containing many more related observations and discussions, and to also be confronted with the most likely historical scenario of what actually happened in our religious past, and then to see how that applies to now, please read The Turning Tide, Volume One, by James D. Littrell. Volume Two should be out sometime in 2008.